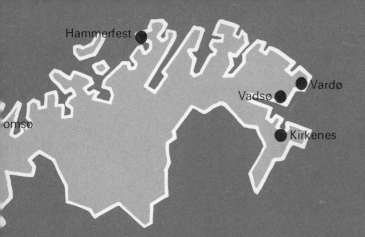

Hammerfest

Vardø

Vadsø

Kirkenes

omsø

NORWAY IN 50 SECONDS

 Population 1972: 3.922 million

 Midnight sun at North Cape 14 May – 29 July

 Main cities 1972: Oslo 477,500
Bergen 212,000
Trondheim 129,000
Stavanger 82,500
Kristiansand 57,700
Drammen 50,200

 100 n. kr. = £ 7.31 = US $ 17.86 (5.9.1973)

 The Royal Family:
HM King Olav V (born 1903)
HRH Crown Prince Harald (born 1937)
HRH Crown Princess Sonja (born 1937)
HRH Prince Haakon Magnus (born 1973)
HRH Princess Märtha Louise (born 1971)
The Princesses Ragnhild (born 1930) and
Astrid (born 1932)
are married to Norwegian citizens.

 Employment by trade:
Agriculture and forestry 11.2%

 Fishing 2.2%

 Industry 36.2%

 Trade 13.5%

 Transport 10.2%

 Other services 26.7%

 Total employment: 1.544 million

 Life expectancy: Men 71.1 years
Women 76.8 years

 Merchant fleet: 2898 ships – 22.1 mill. grt.

Gross National Product 1972: 96 666 mill. kr.
Norway ranks fifth in GNP per capita after USA, Canada, Switzerland and Sweden.
Main trade partners:
Exports: Sweden 18.6%, United Kingdom 18.5%, West Germany 14.8%,
USA 7.9%, Denmark 7.8%.
Imports: Sweden 18.6%, West Germany 14.8%, United Kingdom 13.1%,
Denmark 7.2%, USA 6.7%.

ISBN 82-504-0032-1

Norway's popular monarch, H.M. King
Olav V, celebrated his 70th birthday in
July 1973.

'74 NEW NORWAY

Editor: Gunnar Jerman
Layout: Bjørg Omholt

THE EXPORT COUNCIL OF NORWAY

GRØNDAHL & SØN   OSLO 1973

0527 HRS 0627 HRS 0727 HRS 0827 HRS 0927 HRS 1027 HRS 1127 HRS 1227 HRS 1327 HRS 1427 HRS 1527 HRS

The sun does not sink below the horizon in North Norway from May to July. This exceptional panorama shows the position of the sun during 24 hours in North Norway. The photos were taken at Hekkingen at the mouth of Malangen Fjord, south of Tromsø. Printed with permission from SAS Norway.

© by The Export Council of Norway and Grøndahl & Søn.
Oslo 1973.
Translated by Janet Aagenæs.
Photo-composing,
reproduction and printing
by Grøndahl & Søns Boktrykkeri, Oslo.
Paper from Saugbrugsforeningen, Halden.
Binding by M. Fredriksen.

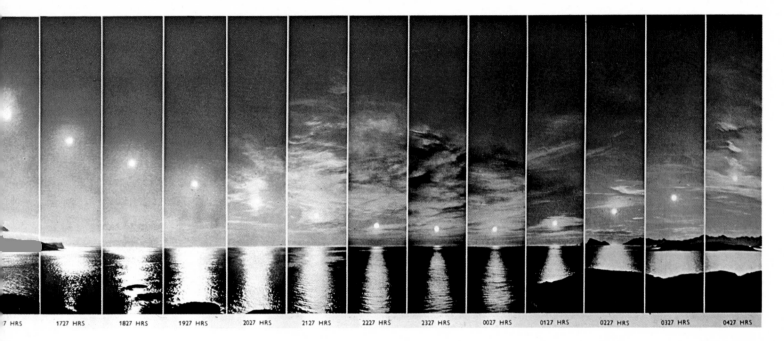

ON THE TOP OF THE WORLD

This solar panorama has appeared in several international magazines, including LIFE. We quote from LIFE:

Throughout the continents of the earth where most of humanity is centered, the pace and pattern of man's living is governed by the endless, changeless rhythm of the rising and setting sun. But in the strange, silent wastelands of the polar regions – literally the ends of the earth – this celestial chronology is weirdly distorted: during the Arctic winter the sun never rises; night runs headlong into night. In summer the sun never sets; dusk is transformed into dawn, and there is no darkness.

Seen side by side, the pictures in this panorama seem to show that the sun rises and falls with a wavelike motion. Actually it does not. If the photographs were arranged to form a cylinder, with the observer on the inside, it would be seen that the sun moves in a perfectly flat but somewhat tilted plane which lies closest to the horizon in the north and highest above it in the south.

The explanation of the Arctic sun's strange travel can be found in three facts about the earth's own motions: 1) that it rotates on a north-south axis once every 24 hours; 2) that it circles the sun once every 365 days, moving in a flat plane which passes through the sun itself, and, 3) that its axis is not perpendicular to this plane but is tilted 23.5° from the perpendicular. It is this slight tilt that brings nightless day to one pole and, simultaneously, dayless night to the other. If the earth's axis were straight up and down, both poles would always be on the line dividing darkness from light and every other point on the globe would get exactly 12 hours of day and 12 of night. There would be no midnight sun and no seasons. But because it is tilted there are two periods during the earth's early circuit when one of the poles is inclined toward the sun and the other away from it.

5

LIVING
WITH THE SEA

Norway is located far to the north of the population centres of Europe. It is difficult to understand how 4 million people can live – so comfortably – in such an unusually elongated country at such high latitudes. This long, narrow country – four miles at its narrowest point – measures 1,100 miles from the North Cape to Lindesnes in the south, and if we could imagine Norway turned around its southernmost point it would reach all the way to Rome.

With a surface area of 124,000 square miles Norway is in terms of size one of the largest countries in Europe (Spitzbergen with 24,000 square miles is not included in this figure). The greater part of this area, however, consists of unproductive mountain regions and the density of population is lower than in most other European countries.

The population is scattered over a land area equal in size to the whole of the British Isles. One third of the country actually lies beyond the Arctic Circle and along the same parallels lie territories steeped in everlasting snow and ice – Greenland, Alaska and Siberia.

It is the sea that makes Norway inhabitable. The temperate climate of this northern outpost is due to the warm currents of the Gulf Stream which flow along the shores of Norway. The Gulf Stream brings fish to spawn in Norwegian waters and ensures that no Norwegian ports are icebound during the winter.

Norway has traditionally been a rugged and demanding country with limited resources. The long cold winters and difficult mountainous terrain have presented considerable challenges to the perseverance, skill and character of the Norwegians.

Most of Norway's population lives less than 12 miles from the sea. The coastline is 12,000 miles long and it is easy to understand why the sea has played such a key role in determining the Norwegians' way of life. Through-out the centuries Norwegians have, by necessity, been seafarers, travelling by boat from one part of the country to another.

The sea made it possible for Norway to become one nation. The high mountains, the deep forests, the narrow valleys and steep hillsides made travelling by land cumbersome. By sea, distances could more easily be over-come. All along the coast, deep fjords wind their way between the mountain ranges, while more than 100,000 islands form the unique Norwegian archipelago – the dream of every Norwegian during the long, dark winter.

The sea has also been Norway's link to the rest of Europe and other parts of the world, and the name Norway, in fact, reflects the ancient fairway to the north.

These conditions provided a natural basis for the development of skills and know-how in all activities related to the sea.

The sea has been Norway's larder ever since people settled there. Norwegian fishing know-how is world renowned and today the country is one of the most important fishery nations in the world. Fish was, in fact, one of Norway's first export products in Viking days. Today, Norwegian fishermen using the most modern vessels and advanced equipment bring in about 3 million tons of fish annually, and a considerable share of the catch is brought to the ultramodern processing plants scattered all along the coast.

The shipping and shipbuilding industries have also thrived on the experience and expertise which Norwegians have gained from their exceptionally close and essential contact with the sea. Shipbuilding has been a highly developed art in Norway ever since the Norwegian Vikings sailed their longships to distant shores thousands of years ago. Craftsmanship and skill in this field have resulted in the design and construction of a wide variety of ships and boats, exported to all parts of the world.

Those engaged in the shipping and shipbuilding industries of Norway have always enjoyed a highly-respected and prestigious position. As a result, these industries have been able to recruit their personnel from among the most highly qualified young people in the country. This has given Norway a competitive advantage which is still unmatched in world shipping. Norwegian seamen, a modern merchant fleet of 1,350 ships totalling more than 22 million tons, managed by Norwegian owners and brokers handle a sizable share of the world's ocean transport requirements.

Norway's geographic location and long coastline probably also provide much of the explanation for Norwegian accomplishments as explorers. The year-long expeditions to the Arctic and Antarctic regions by Fritjof Nansen, Roald Amundsen and others made headlines all over the world in the early part of this century. Thor Heyerdahl's adventures on the Kon Tiki and the papyrus boat «Ra» more recently have reconfirmed the Norwegians' drive to explore the unknown.

The vast Norwegian mountains, seemingly barren and inaccessible, also proved to be an invaluable asset to the country. The water rushing down from the 165,000 mountain lakes and glaciers created the basis for producing hydro-electric power. The harnessing of economical and plentiful electricity made it possible to develop a modern and competitive industry producing ferro-alloys, aluminium and other metals. Norway has the greatest resources of hydro-electric power of all European countries. Around half of the available hydro-electric power resources has been exploited.

The Norwegian economy is to a very high degree based on the exchange of goods and services with foreign countries. In 1972 the export of goods and services accounted for 41 per cent of the GNP. Even if few countries have a larger foreign trade in relation to their GNP, it cannot be said that Norway has a unique position in this respect. A large exchange of goods and services with foreign countries is typical of small countries with a highly developed economy.

Today, Norway has reached a level of economic development which compares favourably to the most highly industrialized countries in the world. Yet, the future seems to hold even greater challenges and opportunities. Major oil and gas deposits have been found in the Norwegian sector of the continental shelf in the North Sea. This will undoubtedly lead to unprecedented economic growth, but will also entail sizable problems.

These new and unexpected riches hidden in the sea off Norway's coast will make Norway the first significant oil exporter of Europe. This will be part of the far-reaching economic changes that Norway is facing.

At the threshold to this new era, politicians, the authorities, and business leaders are seeking ways to use these new resources for the further development and benefit of this northernmost European country.

We hope that this edition of New Norway will illustrate some of the many aspects of life and conditions in Norway today – as well as some of the prospects for the future.

Left: Tromsø – more than 185 miles north of the Arctic Circle is called «the gateway to the Arctic Ocean». The town is the largest in North Norway and the site of the country's new university.
Above: A winter day in Oslo.

9

FOCUS ON PEOPLE

The difficult living conditions have through the ages represented a continuous challenge to those who live and work in Norway and Norway's history is the story of how a people met the challenges and mastered them. Traces of human activity found in Finnmark indicate that people inhabited the area 9,000 years ago. They based their existence on the resources which were found in the sea, the forests and the mountains, as Norwegians have done to this day.

Of course, special problems do arise when such a small population is scattered over a large area, as in Norway. Living conditions vary from one region to another and the resources have never been equally distributed. In general, however, it has been possible to overcome the difficulties which have arisen, and it is hardly incorrect to say that Norway today enjoys greater equality and has fewer areas of conflict than perhaps any other country.

Some of the most serious social conflicts in the world stem from differences in race, religion and language. Norway has small and few minority groups. The 20,000 Lapps represent the most important group from a social and cultural point of view. The Lapps have lived in Norway for several thousand years; they have their own language and 10 per cent of them are still nomads tending reindeer herds. Most Lapps, however, are fishermen and smallholders.

There are no other ethnic minority groups in Norway. More than 96 per cent of the population belongs to the State Church. Norway is a country where just about everyone speaks and understands the national language. There is one national school system, one set of institutions for higher education and one broadcasting corporation. There are also few foreigners employed in Norway, except in the merchant marine.

Many foreigners associate Norway with fishing, whaling and forestry, believing that these activities represent the cornerstone of the Norwegian economy. This is not a true picture of the situation in Norway today. Less than 13 per cent of the working population is employed in the primary industries and the figure is declining rapidly. The service industries employ about half of the working population, while every third member of the labour force is employed by manufacturing industry.

Norwegian children thrive outdoors in close contact with nature.
Practical clothing, like rainwear made by Helly-Hansen, makes it just as popular to play outdoors when it's wet or snowy.

Unemployment has been virtually non-existent in Norway since World War II. The working population totals more than 1.6 million people and the figure is increasing slowly compared to the tasks ahead. This results in a considerable pressure on the labour market and hampers the development in many fields. Modern Norway is characterized by full employment and a keen competition for manpower. Labour-management relations have been remarkably peaceful since the 1930s and there have been no major strikes during recent decades. Still, thanks to strong organisations and legislation, wage-earners have managed to attain considerable results in the form of social benefits, higher wages and co-determination in their companies. A pension scheme for the entire population has been implemented and the social security system is well-developed. Education is free and a system of student loans brings a university education within the reach of all.

More and more young people are obtaining a higher education. The average child spends 11.5 years in school before he enters the labour market. This situation entails that the working population is increasing at a slow rate, currently less than 1 per cent annually. Women account for the only manpower reserve of importance in the Norwegian society today.

Right: Norsk Lettmetall, Europe's largest producer of power lawn mowers, is among the modern manufacturing industries in Norway today.

Below: Yesterday and today in the Norwegian engineering industry, where women are beginning to play an active role. Nylands Verksted in Oslo.

Bottom: Maritime traditions have produced experts in all fields related to the sea. The photo is from Haugesund Mek. Verksted which will deliver a series of 12 special tankers to Shell and Mobil by 1976.

Next page: Norway's electric power consumption is far higher per capita than anywhere else in the world. The harnessing of water power resources has made Norwegian contractors and suppliers of equipment the specialists in this field.

14

Fishing has taken place along the coast since man first settled in Norway. Fishing and mining are, in fact, the oldest economic activities in the country. Tradition and experience have made Norway one of the world's largest fishery nations and each year close to 3 million tons of fish are brought to the processing plants scattered along the coast. Most of the catch is processed before being exported to the world markets.

Mining is less important to the Norwegian economy, but many valuable minerals and ores are extracted from Norway's mountains : almost 4 million tons of iron ore, 450,000 tons of ilmenite from Europe's largest ilmenite deposits, copper and pyri-

tes which are mined together, as well as zinc, lead and nepheline-syenite.

Top right: A woman in a man's world. Grete Lill Jensen, 25, Norway's first woman marine engineer.

16

Top:

Far left: Electronics is a new speciality where Norwegian industry has made outstanding progress, internationally as well.

Left: Crossing a fjord on the west coast with a high tension line is a difficult task. The new explosive method of compression jointing from A/S Raufoss Ammunisjonsfabrikker makes the task easier.

Below: Close to 700 of the Kværner Group's 5,700 employees are gradunate engineers. Power plant equipment is one of the company's specialities. The photo shows the world's most powerful Pelton turbine produced by the Kværner Group.

Left: Norway has made great progress in the chemical industry and many of the products from this sector are being produced under licence abroad.

In creating products for the home Norwegian designers have succeeded in combining traditional craftsmanship with industrial requirements. The photos on these pages are from David Andersen A/S, a leading jewellery and silverware producer, and Sandvika Veveri, a firm producing textile specialities. On the next page we see a design by Hadelands Glassverk, one of Europe's oldest glassworks established in 1762. The «Tangen» goblet, shown here, is a true reproduction of a design that Hadelands Glassverk has been making since the 18th century.

NEW RESOURCES FROM THE SEA BED

When the Ekofisk field is in full production in a few years, Norway can expect to see an oil production far in excess of the country's current requirement. The discoveries already made will make Norway the only net exporter of hydrocarbons in Western Europe. There is also reason to believe that additional discoveries will be made which will strengthen Norway's new position as an oil nation. The discoveries which have already been made in the Ekofisk and Frigg fields will, during the years of peak production, yield oil, condensate and gas totalling 50 million tons of oil equivalents on an annual basis. This figure does not take into account finds which are not yet evaluated, such as Edda, Eldfisk and Heimdal, and certainly not new finds which presumably will be made in the same areas and in new oil-producing areas not yet identified. The real production figures will therefore be considerably higher.

50 million tons annually is, of course, not a great deal compared to European oil consumption or production in the Middle East. But it is overwhelming when related to Norwegian conditions. It is equivalent to 6–7 times the Norwegian oil consumption or about 3 times the country's total energy consumption.

All the discoveries made thus far are located close to the important European markets. Aerial magnetic and seismic surveys are providing good indications of the prospects for new finds. This has made the North Sea one of the most attractive areas in the world for offshore oil prospecting.

The oil fever which gripped Norway at the beginning of the 1970s will probably continue for some years to come. At the same time that new oil and gas discoveries on the Norwegian continental shelf demonstrate that Norway is in the process of becoming an important oil nation, Norwegian industry is actively preparing for the new challenges and possibilities created by the new oil activities off the coast of Norway. Norwegian enterprises are involved in major projects related to all aspects of the oil industry. Norsk Hydro and other Norwegian groups are already participating in the oil adventure through part ownership in the Ekofisk, Eldfisk, Tor, Heimdal and Frigg fields. Recently established oil companies are becoming involved in oil exploration and Norwegian shipowners have contracted one of the world's largest fleets of oil drilling rigs as well as 24 supply ships for service in the North Sea.

Photo: The Ekofisk field.

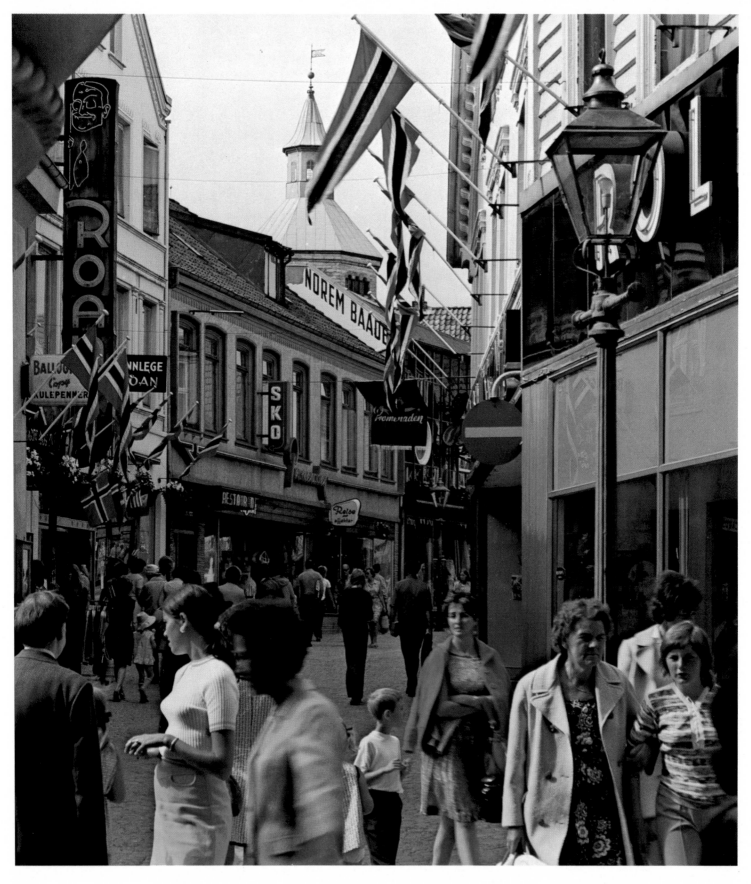

Opposite: Church Street, Stavanger. Stavanger is the centre of Norwegian oil activities. The Norwegian State Oil Company – Statoil – and the Oil Directorate have established their headquarters in this old but active North Sea town.

Right: The basis for the oil adventure: samples and crude oil from Ekofisk.

Below: The most important discoveries on the Norwegian continental shelf have been made close to the British sector. In several cases the discoveries extend across both British and Norwegian territory.

Next page left: The enormous oil storage caisson which now rests on the bottom of the North Sea – is here being towed to its

final destination. The tank, with a capacity of one million barrels of oil, has been built by the Norwegian contractors Høyer-Ellefsen A/S and F. Selmer A/S, and represents Norway's largest contribution to the «Ekofisk town» thus far. The tank is made of reinforced and prestressed concrete. Now resting on the seabed, it looms 65 feet above sea level and provides over 170,000 sq.ft. of platform space. In addition to serving as a reservoir for oil, the tank's steel decks will provide space for production facilities for fields in the area as well as equipment for the pipeline systems.

Next pages right: Yet another new oil discovery in the North Sea.

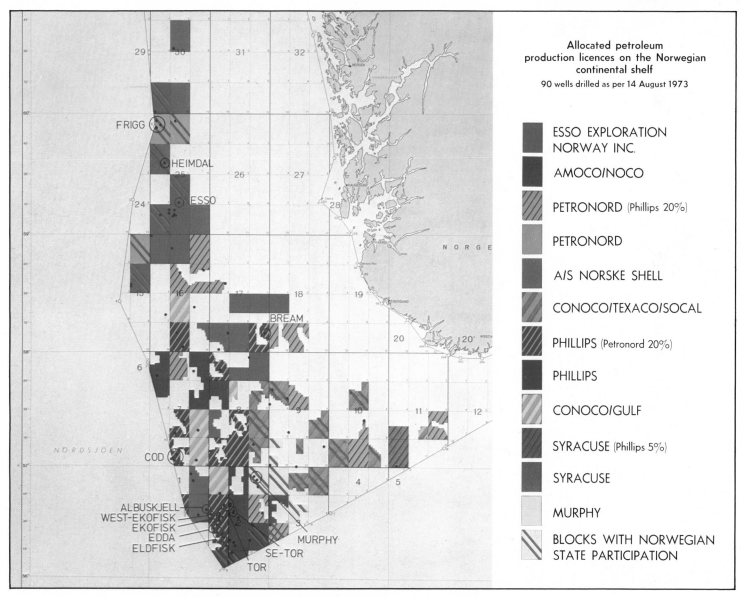

Allocated petroleum
production licences on the Norwegian
continental shelf
90 wells drilled as per 14 August 1973

ESSO EXPLORATION NORWAY INC.

AMOCO/NOCO

PETRONORD (Phillips 20%)

PETRONORD

A/S NORSKE SHELL

CONOCO/TEXACO/SOCAL

PHILLIPS (Petronord 20%)

PHILLIPS

CONOCO/GULF

SYRACUSE (Phillips 5%)

SYRACUSE

MURPHY

BLOCKS WITH NORWEGIAN STATE PARTICIPATION

Drilling and exploration activities are more expensive and more demanding in the North Sea than anywhere else. Not only have the oil finds been made in water depths of over 250–300 feet, but they have also been generally discovered at considerable distances from the coast. The weather conditions in the winter are also extremely rough. Still, enormous amounts are being invested, and it is expected that 50 oil rigs will be operating in the North Sea in 1974.

By the summer of 1973, 78 wells at a total cost of $250 million had been drilled on the Norwegian continental shelf south of the 62nd parallel.

Thus far only 20 per cent of the North Sea has been explored and even in this area further exploration is required to ascertain the full economic value of oil and gas resources.

Photo: Working on the drilling platforms in the North Sea is no bed of roses. Continuous waves of 75 feet and more are not unknown, while the winds can reach 100 m.p.h. The crews generally work 14 days on board followed by 14 days off ashore. It is still too early to predict the true magnitude of oil and gas resources on the Norwegian continental shelf and in the North Sea. The estimates are continuously being revised upwards and for this reason it is impossible to calculate Norway's future oil revenue. Is is obvious, however, that the North Sea oil will alter the economic structure of the country. A conservative estimate indicates that the Norwegian State will have an annual income of about $500–$800 million at the end of the 1970s.

Scenes from the North Sea.
The 217-mile pipeline which will carry crude oil from Ekofisk to Teesside in England will have a diameter of 34 inches. Initially, the pipeline will be able to transport 35,000 barrels of oil a day, but in two years' time the volume is expected to increase to a million barrels daily.

The photo this page left shows the pipeline being laid. It is envisaged that it will be in operation in September 1974.

In April 1974 work will begin on the gas pipeline from Ekofisk to Emden in West Germany. This will be completed in 1975. The pipeline, with a diameter of 36 inches, will ultimately have a total capacity of 2,500 million cubic feet a day.

According to plans, other oil fields in the Ekofisk area will be brought into this oil and gas pipeline system.

Above: From the production platform on Ekofisk.

Norwegian owners have thus far ordered a total of 16 drilling platforms and 1 drillship. The new rigs represent a total investment of between $270–$300 million and will require a crew of about 1,000 men. Norway is the biggest builder of oil drilling platforms in Europe and ranks second on a world basis after the U.S. In summer 1973 rigs under construction and on order in Norway for Norwegian and American owners numbered fourteen, of which ten of the Aker Group's H-3 design.

Right: A model of an Aker H-3 platform was tested in the ship model experimental tank at Wageningen, the Netherlands. Very good motion characteristics in dril-

ling conditions were achieved. The survival test proved that the platform performed well even in waves of 100 feet.

Above: The first Aker H-3 Drilling Platform under construction at the new Verdal yard.

Opposite page:
Bottom right: The Normarig Group with headquarters in Brevik is also building oil rigs. The photo shows the work on the pontoons on the first platform being built by the group.

This page:
Left: The construction of the pontoons for the first Aker H-3 platform at Aker Verdal A/S.

Below: There is oil activity in the centre of the capital as well. «Ocean Voyager» being completed at the Nylands yard just outside the Oslo town hall.

The preceding pages will have demonstrated clearly that it is not Norway's intention simply to sit back and collect royalties and taxes from the oil companies; on the contrary, the country intends to guide the development and participate in all activities related to the oil industry.

One possibility is the establishment of a Norwegian petrochemical industry. The development in this field is still at the planning stage, but a number of major industrial groups are involved in the preparations. Norsk Hydro and Norsk Brændselolje are already in the process of building a new oil refinery at Mongstad, north of Bergen. 2,000 construction workers will ensure that the plant is ready for operation in the spring of 1975.

Below: Mongstad as it appeared in 1972.

Right: Mongstad as it is expected to appear in 1975. The photo shows an oil refinery already in operation in Norway, the Shell refinery near Stavanger.

The supply service for the rigs and production platforms in the North Sea is very important and a number of supply bases have been established on the Norwegian coast. The Aker Group's Norsco base and North Sea Exploration Service's base, both near Stavanger, are two of the largest and most advanced in the North Sea area. The photos on these pages are from the Norsco base. In the middle of the 1960s the entire area was nothing but heather fields and wilderness. Today, it is a modern supply centre with 30 foreign companies as tenants and 250 employees who are specialists in all areas of service for the oil industry.

The Norsco base will remain the main

base for the Aker Group in the years ahead, but the Group is also planning to establish supply bases near Bergen, at Møre, in North Norway, and on the Shetland Islands in cooperation with a British company.

Right: Sandblasting of anchor chains for oil platforms.

Above: Specialists handle the assignments.

34

Top: Pipes for the Ekofisk field are being inspected with x-ray equipment by an engineer from Det norske Veritas.

Below: Pipes for transporting oil from the production platform to the storage tank on the Ekofisk field are being loaded on the world's largest floating crane, «Choctaw». Each pipe weighs 60 tons and is welded together into large sections on the base, x-rayed and pressure tested, and covered by a concrete casing in order to save time in the field.

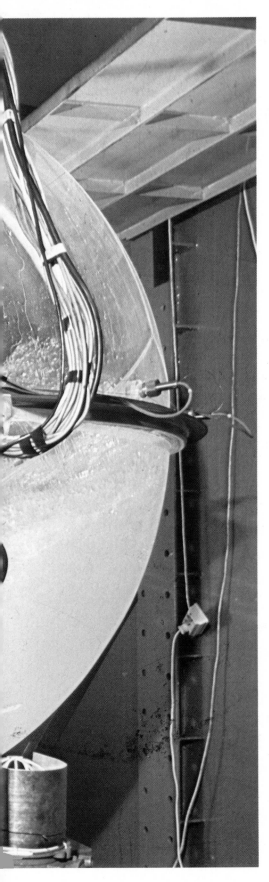

A NATION
OF SHIPBUILDERS

Ever since men first settled on Norway's long and convoluted shore, boats have been built there. Traces of boatyards go back to Viking days and earlier. Today there are still hundreds of boatyards and a score of shipyards building all kinds of vessels, including mammoth tankers and sophisticated gas carriers.

With one of the world's largest merchant fleets, and with a shipbuilding industry that ranks among the world's «Top Ten», Norway has naturally developed marine equipment as an engineering speciality. This is a field where Norway has a broad-based home market, including fishing vessels as well as merchant ships, and where a close contact with owners and operators, designers and builders, has inspired engineers to develop new and advanced products aimed at improved safety and efficiency. Shipping – under free trade conditions – is possibly the most competitive branch of commercial enterprise, and marine equipment that is efficient and economical, robust and reliable, is vital to ensure successful operations.

Norwegian shipbuilding today is a major export industry. The Norwegian shipyards are being expanded at a rate which is arousing international attention. The Aker Group has just completed its large series of 220,000-ton tankers and has now started on a new series of 285,000-tonners. Even this, however, is not a limit for the size of ships that the Group shall build in the future. The Kværner Group's patented liquefied natural gas carriers are being built under licence in many parts of the world. Yards all over the country are building series of specialized ships for Norwegian and foreign owners. Actually, there are about 100 yards in Norway building and launching a variety of small and large ships for use on the Seven Seas. In addition the construction of oil-drilling platforms and supply ships represents an important new activity for Norwegian shipyards.

Photo: Spherical tanks for LNG carriers are being tested by the Research Department of Det norske Veritas, on behalf of Moss-Rosenberg Verft A/S. The photo shows tests of stress on the internal structure as the result of ship movement and changes in the quantity of gas held by the tank. The full-scale tanks will carry liquefied natural gas at a temperature of – 162 °C.

37

In the new and rapidly expanding field of gas carriers. Norwegian shipbuilders have played a pioneering role, and Moss-Rosenberg Verft A/S, with yards at Moss and Stavanger, has an important international position in this field.

The Moss-Rosenberg patented gas carriers are built under licence by leading shipyards abroad, including Mitsubishi, Mitsui and Kawasaki in Japan, General Dynamics in the U.S., Astilleros Espanoles in Spain, Italcantieri in Italy, and Howaldtswerke-Deutsche Werft in Germany.

Opposite: An LNG carrier with the patented spherical tank design being built at the Rosenberg yard. The ship, which was built for British shipowners, has a capacity of 87,600 cubic metres.

This page: Norwegian manufacturers are active in supplying equipment to the gas carriers. The photo to the left shows propellers from A. M. Liaaen, Ålesund. The gas 'tower' below, supplied by Nordisk Aluminiumindustri, has a length of 104 feet. There is a pipe in the tower used for filling the tank and a spiral staircase leading to the bottom.

Next pages: Night at the dock of the Moss yard. An LNG carrier with a capacity of 29,000 cubic metres cooled liquid gas is being completed.

39

About 150 marine equipment manufacturers in Norway are exporting to yards and shipowners abroad as well as supplying Norway's own needs. In a number of fields they have pioneered new products, such as hydraulic deck machinery, steering machines and controllable pich propellers.

A considerable number of Norwegian products in the field of ships' gear are being manufactured under licence in other countries. Hydraulic deck machines from Norway have been delivered to vessels in 30 countries. At Japanese yards 75 per cent of all newbuildings are equipped with deck machines made under licence from A/S Hydraulic Brattvaag or Norwinch.

Opposite page:

Top: Skill and know-how are required to produce propellers.

Bottom: Seven Norwegian companies manufacture diesel engines. A/S Horten Verft produces engines up to 35,000 BHP under licence from Sulzer Brothers Ltd., Switzerland.

This page:

Left: Norwinch anchor windlass for 108 mm chain being produced at A/S Bergen Mekaniske Verksteder for later delivery to a 227,000 dwt. OBO ship being built in West Germany. BMV is a member of the Aker Group.

Above: A Bergen diesel auxiliary engine being hoisted aboard the 285,000-ton turbine tanker «Fabian». See the following pages. Bergens Mekaniske Verksteder has produced more than 3,000 engines since they started production 28 years ago, and is now one of the world's largest manufacturers of diesel engines for ships.

In 1972 the Aker Group delivered the first of a series of 285,000-ton tankers from its Stord yard. The ship, named «Fabian», was built for the shipowner Hilmar Reksten. In the spring of 1973 the Aker Group had 16 VLCC (very large crude carriers) on order. Five ships of 370,000 tons were on order in addition to the series of 285,000 tonners.

Stord yard, located in West Norway, is a good example of the growing industrialization in some rural areas in Norway. The district, highly interesting from an historical point of view, has rich traditions in the shipbuilding field. The oldest ship found in Norway was built in this district almost 2,000 years ago and the remains of a small boatyard dating back to the 5th century were discovered during the construction of the new dock for supertankers.

The photos on these pages are from the construction of «Fabian». The ship has an overall length of about 1,130 feet (347 metres). It was built in two sections which were launched separately and then welded together at the quay.

Opposite page.
Top right: Section being towed from the Aker Group yard at Kragerø, South Norway to Stord.

Bottom right: Stem part leaving the dock to join stern part at the outfitting quay.

This page. Above: The two parts ready for welding together.

Left: «Fabian» on her way to the Persian Gulf.

Horten Verft and Haugesund mek. Verksted (photos this page) represent two Norwegian shipyards with considerable foreign orders. The Haugesund yard completed a series of eight 23,700-ton bulk carriers for owners in Scotland in 1972 and has now started building a series of eleven 32,000-ton parcel tankers for Mobil and Shell. The Horten yard has also specialized in parcel tankers and is building 8 ships for British owners.

The photos on this page provide a few examples of the equipment being produced by the 150 Norwegian ships' gear manufacturers actively exporting to all parts of the world.

Top: The largest nozzle propellers in the world, delivered to a 213,000-ton tanker built in Japan. The equipment is designed and produced by A/S Strømmen Staal. The company has a licence agreement with Kawasaki Heavy Industries Ltd., Japan for the production of nozzles in the Far East.

Below left: Hydraulic 16-ton deck cranes on board a 24,000-ton bulk carrier.

Below right: Telescopic accommodation ladder from Marine Aluminium installed on board a 230,000-ton supertanker.

Bottom: Harding covered lifeboat – now being installed on a number of drilling platforms and drilling vessels.

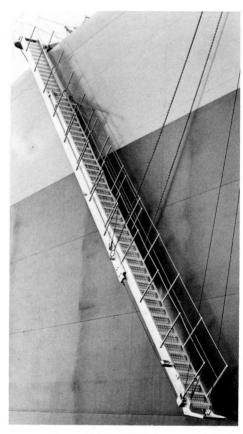

«Intelligence industry» is Norway's name for the rapidly growing production of electronic equipment and systems. This is a field where extraordinary progress has been made in relatively few years. Measured by the standards of the giant corporations in other countries, the Norwegian companies in this sphere are small. Nevertheless, they are proving competitive, even on the international market.

Norwegian electronics engineers have concentrated on applying the new technology to fields of activity where Norway has special know-how and long traditions. This includes such fields as shipping and fishing.

A/S Kongsberg Våpenfabrikk, located in Kongsberg 60 miles from Oslo, is a leading manufacturer of products ranging from car parts to gas turbines, rockets, weapon systems and electronic navigation systems. The KV data processing programme, control units and drafting machines are used in shipbuilding as well as automotive and aircraft industries throughout the world.

The photos on the top of these pages show a Kongsberg drafting machine with a computer control unit (opposite page) and the special clean room at Kongsberg, mainly used for assembling parts with tolerances down to 3/1000 of a millimetre.

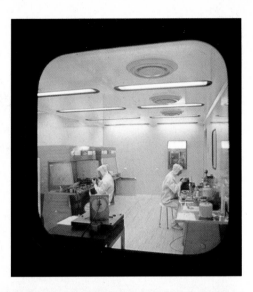

Noratom-Norcontrol has delivered about 50 per cent of the anti-collision systems in use onboard ships. The DataBridge anti-collision and navigation system is installed in ships built in Norway, U. S. A., U.K., Japan, Sweden and the U.S.S.R. The world's biggest shipbuilding group, IHI in Japan, will manufacture Data-Bridge under licence from Noratom-Norcontrol. Norcontrol has also developed the AutoChief and DataChief systems for engine room automation. Autochief is a main engine bridge control system. Data-Chief is a new computer-controlled system for engine room control. The first unit was installed in a 280,000-ton tanker built in Japan in 1972. Complete systems for pe-

riodically unmanned engine rooms have been delivered not only to newbuildings, but also to ships in service with the installation carried out during normal ship operations in order to avoid delays.

Left: The first computer-controlled Data-Chief unit being tested before shipment to Japan.

Above: AutoChief II engine control system, showing one of the new integrated circuit cards.

ARCTIC MINING

Norway's vast coastline is notched with fjords and inlets which are flanked by towering mountains and steep slopes. The mountains, which cover about 70 per cent of Norway's land area, are more than just harsh and windblown barren regions. They also contain resources which have been exploited by Norwegians for centuries. Mining is, in fact, one of the oldest industrial activities in the country.

The first iron ore was extracted 2,000 years ago, but the first three major mines in Norway were not actually started until the 17th century. These same mines were in operation until relatively recently and their history records the saga of man's struggle with nature and fluctuating economic conditions. When companies like Kongsberg Sølvverk and Røros Kobberverk experienced their peak periods they were among the most important and largest in the country, and throughout their several hundred years of existence, periods of prosperity and progress alternated with periods of adversity and disappointment.

Iron ore, copper and pyrites are the most important ore deposits found in Norway. The centre of Norwegian mining operations is located in North Norway. In this area we find the iron ore mines in Sør-Varanger and the Dunderland Valley, the copper mines in Repparfjord, Biddjovagge and Sulitjelma and the nepheline deposits on the island of Stjernøy.

Mines are also worked in other parts of the country. The ore, seldom rich, usually contains little metal in relation to the quantity of stone quarried. Many mountain regions are yet to be explored and intense prospecting is being carried out today to find out whether additional ore resources exist in Norway.

The most exciting and fascinating mining community in Norway is found in the Arctic archipelago of Svalbard (Spitzbergen). Coal mining has been carried on there during most of this century. Svalbard means «the cool coast», but a branch of the Gulf Stream flows along the western and northern coast of Spitzbergen and during the summer months keeps the sea ice free further north than any other part of the world.

Left: Bjørnøya, one of the Svalbard islands but completely isolated from the others, lies more than 250 miles away from the Norwegian coast. The polar bear has given the island its name. Coal was also mined here at one time.

More than 400,000 tons of coal are shipped annually from Store Norske Spitsbergen Kullkompani's mines in Longyearbyen, Spitzbergen. The shipping season is short and hectic because the harbour is icebound during the winter months. Spitzbergen has a fascinating topography and climate, but the sharp contrast between summer and winter has a major influence on working conditions. On Spitzbergen there are more than 100 days when the sun does not rise above the horizon, but of course equally many days with the Midnight Sun.

Left: Fossils from Spitzbergen's fertile past.

Below: A winter night in Longyearbyen.

Right: Hunting and fishing represented the only basis for economic activities on Spitzbergen until the beginning of this century. The animal most people associate with the Arctic region is the polar bear. His world is floating ice where he finds his most important nourishment – the seal. More characteristic and perhaps more spectacular, however, is the birdlife found on Svalbard. Millions of birds converge on the islands for the breeding season during the summer, but only one spends the winter – the ptarmigan.

Even during the winter the working conditions inside the mines are ideal with an average temperature of – 3°C. While the mines in southern regions are often located far below the surface, the situation on Spitzbergen is different. The miners must climb the side of the mountain to enter the mines. In addition to the Norwegian mining operations in Longyearbyen, the Russians are also mining on Svalbard.

Except for the small crews manning the observation stations and some hunters, only the miners and their families stay through the winter. The miners often combine winter employment on Spitzbergen with farming in North Norway during the summer.

More than half of Svalbard's surface is covered by inland ice and in some areas the arms of the glaciers reach all the way down to the coast. In spite of all the snow and ice the vegetation is amazingly rich, considering the fact that it is located only 10–12 degrees of latitude away from the North Pole. The abundance of flowers makes an overwhelming impression amidst the barren wilderness. The flowers that grow there, representing 140 plant species, are many in number but small in size. However, no trees are found except for some stunted dwarf birch.

This page: Up to now coal deposits have been the main economic resource of the archipelago of Svalbard (Spitzbergen). Intensive explorations and seismic surveys, however, have strengthened the belief that gas and oil resources may exist in this harsh Polar region. Several expeditions have been made to investigate the area and one major oil drilling project is also in progress.

Opposite page: A new and interesting mining operation has started up on the island of Stjernøy in the far north of Norway. There, Norsk Nefelin – part of the Elkem-Spigerverket Group – produces nepheline syenite, used as a raw material in the glass and porcelain industries.
The deposits on Stjernøy contain several hundred millions tons.

One of the most recent mining operations to be started in Norway is located near Hjerkinn where the installations are dimensioned for extracting 700,000 tons of crude ore annually. The mine is supplying flotation pyrites to one of Europe's largest sulphuric acid plants built by A/S Borregaard in Sarpsborg.

A mining community has also sprung up in Biddjovagge (below) on the wild expanses of the Finnmark plateau in the northernmost part of Norway. The community is located at an altitude of 2,100 feet above sea level and 25 windblown miles from the closest town – Kautokeino. The obstacles to be overcome to start mining operations at Biddjovagge were overwhel-

ming, but their success represents additional evidence of the pioneering spirit that has always prevailed in Norwegian mining. Even during our age of technology mining operations in Norway are continuously struggling against nature, the cold, periods of darkness and heavy snowfalls. Biddjovagge is still another example of man's eternal struggle against the elements.

Right: Cupreous pyrites.

Two new copper mining installations were completed in Norway in 1972. A new flotation plant and open-pit mine for copper pyrites were started in Repparfjord in Finnmark, Norway's northernmost county. The plant, owned by Folldal Verk A/S, a division of the Borregaard Group, will have an annual production capacity of 8–12,000 tons of copper concentrates. The concentrate contains about 50 per cent pure copper.

A new mine established by Grong Gruber A/S was opened in Trøndelag. The mining will be initially concentrated at the Joma deposits, estimated to hold 16 million tons of pyrites ore. The company expects an annual yield of 18,000 tons of copper concentrates and 4,000 tons of zinc concentrates. The total production from the new mines will be exported.

Left: The crushing plant in Repparfjord.

Below·right: The copper flower (Viscaria alpina) thrives in Repparfjord's cupreous soil.

At Bjørnevatn near Kirkenes in the extreme north-east of Norway, close to the Russian border, a giant hole has been blasted, hundreds of feet deep. This is Norway's biggest iron ore mine (right).

A/S Sydvaranger started mining operations there in 1906 in the most unpropitious circumstances – an Arctic climate, a remote situation, and a low-grade ore with only 30 per cent iron. However, the deposits are extensive, and can be exploited by open-pit mining.

The ore is crushed in a primary crusher and then transported about 4 miles by railway to Kirkenes. In the concentrator at Kirkenes the ore is upgraded to a concentrate containing 65–68 per cent of iron. About fifty per cent of the concentrate is pelletized, while the rest is exported as sinterfeed. The pelletizing plant was completed in 1970. A/S Sydvaranger is going to invest about $33 million in new installations, including a second pellets plant. When the new installations are completed, pellet output will be 2 million tons a year.

Reserves at Bjørnevatn are considered sufficient to continue open-cast mining on the present scale for another 20 to 30 years.

In spite of being situated at latitude 70 North, the Gulf Stream along the Norwegian coast keeps the harbour open for traffic all year round.

Below: Kirkenes has an ice-free harbour all year round. The town is located at 70 North and 30 East, as far north as the northernmost parts of Siberia and Alaska, as far east as Istanbul.

SMELTING THE MOUNTAINS

The claim can be made that Norway was transformed into an industrialized nation by means of its mountains. The enormous mountain plateaus, combined with abundant precipitation, form the basis of an annual production of hydro-electricity, second in Europe only to Soviet production. Industry takes 65 per cent of this power, with the electrochemical and electrometallurgical industries sharing almost 50 per cent of the production total.

The development of an internationally important metallurgical industry in this Arctic country of four million inhabitants, separated by vast oceans from most of the necessary raw material sources, was possible and profitable due to the relative ease with which nature could be exploited for power. The fulfillment of ambitious expansion programmes in Norwegian metallurgy thus depends to a great extent on the nation's ability to keep hydro-power prices at a competitive level.

The most spectacular industrial developments in Norway have been in aluminium. Aluminium production in Norway started more than 50 years ago with the inauguration of two British smelters in 1907 and 1908, but it wasn't until after the Second World War that the expansion began to make tremendous headway. Today, aluminium is Norway's largest export product with an export value of about $330 million. There are 9 aluminium plants in operation, all located in remote rural districts. In addition, there are three major companies involved in aluminium processing and another 1,000 Norwegian companies use aluminium in varying degrees in their production.

Other metals are also very important to Norway's economy, and in the field of ferro-alloys Norway plays a major role internationally. About 93 per cent of the entire ferro-alloy production is shipped abroad. With this marked export-orientation, it is only natural that plants were built on sites along the coast to facilitate shipments to the international markets.

Norway is also the Western world's second largest producer of the light metal magnesium. Norsk Hydro is supplying 16 per cent of world consumption. Biggest single customer is Volkswagen in West Germany.

Photo: From Norsk Hydro's aluminium plant on the island of Karmøy, West Norway.

In 1850 Emperor Napoleon III used dinner plates which were more costly than gold. They were made of aluminium. Today, aluminium is used by everyone. Total world consumption is 8 million tons annually. The annual capacity of the Norwegian aluminium industry alone amounts to more than 700,000 tons and only the U.S. and Canada can boast a larger production. Only Canada ranks ahead of Norway in aluminium exports.

Left: The aluminium plant owned jointly by Elkem-Spigerverket and Alcoa in Mosjøen near the Arctic Circle has an annual capacity of 90,000 tons. The Group has also built a new aluminium smelter in the southern part of Norway.

Below: In connection with the expansion of Årdal Verk, a 53-mile long power line was built from Sogndal to Årdal. The transmission towers pass four districts and difficult mountain terrain with an altitude of 3,600 feet above sea level at the highest point. For the first time in Norway Norwegian-manufactured aluminium power masts were used. They were flown to their various locations by helicopter.

Norsk Hydro's plant on the island of Karmøy near Haugesund is the only Norwegian smelter which is entirely Norwegian-owned. Production capacity amounts to 120,000 tons but the more than half-mile long pot-room has been built with a view to expanding capacity to an annual production of 200,000 tons. The photos on this page are from Karmøy.

Årdal og Sunndal Verk is Norway's largest aluminium producer with an annual capacity of 325,000 tons. The company is owned jointly by the Norwegian State and Alcan Aluminium Limited, Canada. Årdal og Sunndal has ownership interests in a number of aluminium processing companies and aims at processing more of the metal in Norway into semis and finished products.

Photo: Årdalstangen, the port of Årdal Verk, the largest production unit in Europe with an annual production of 170,000 tons.

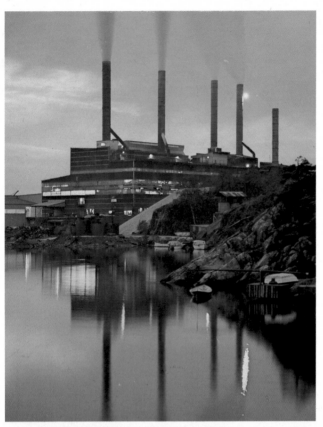

Elkem-Spigerverket is one of the world's largest producers and exporters of ferro-alloys. The alloys are used in the steel and metals industry. Production takes place at four plants: Bremanger, Fiskaa in Kristiansand *(left)*, Porsgrunn and Salten.

Elkem-Spigerverket is a specialist in the field of electric smelting furnaces *(below)* and has recently won a world name for its anti-pollution melting processes. There are now more than 260 Elkem furnaces in operation or under construction throughout the world. In 1972 a delegation from the U.S. Environmental Protection Agency visited Porsgrunn to study an Elkem-Spigerverket furnace of a new closed type. The delegation also visited the aluminium smelter at Lista, known for its effective anti-pollution devices.

Photo. Right: A ferro-silicon furnace at Fiskaa Verk during the smelting process. When in operation the point of the electrode in a FeSi furnace is surrounded by an open, gas-filled space. The electrode and the walls are so hot that they are self-luminous and an arc formed between the electrode and the bottom provides additional light. This makes it possible to photograph the point of the electrode while the furnace is in operation.

In the photo we see the point of the electrode in the upper part of the gas-filled space surrounding it. The electricity load is normal and the arc has the normal appearance for high load. In the foreground we see an unmelted area with metal drops which have been splattered there.

How, it may be asked, did the photographer manage to take the picture without being melted along with the quartz? He did it by peering through a peephole in a laboratory furnace. A hole was made in the furnace and a hollow graphite pipe was inserted into the space around the point of the electrode. The picture could then be taken by using special equipment.

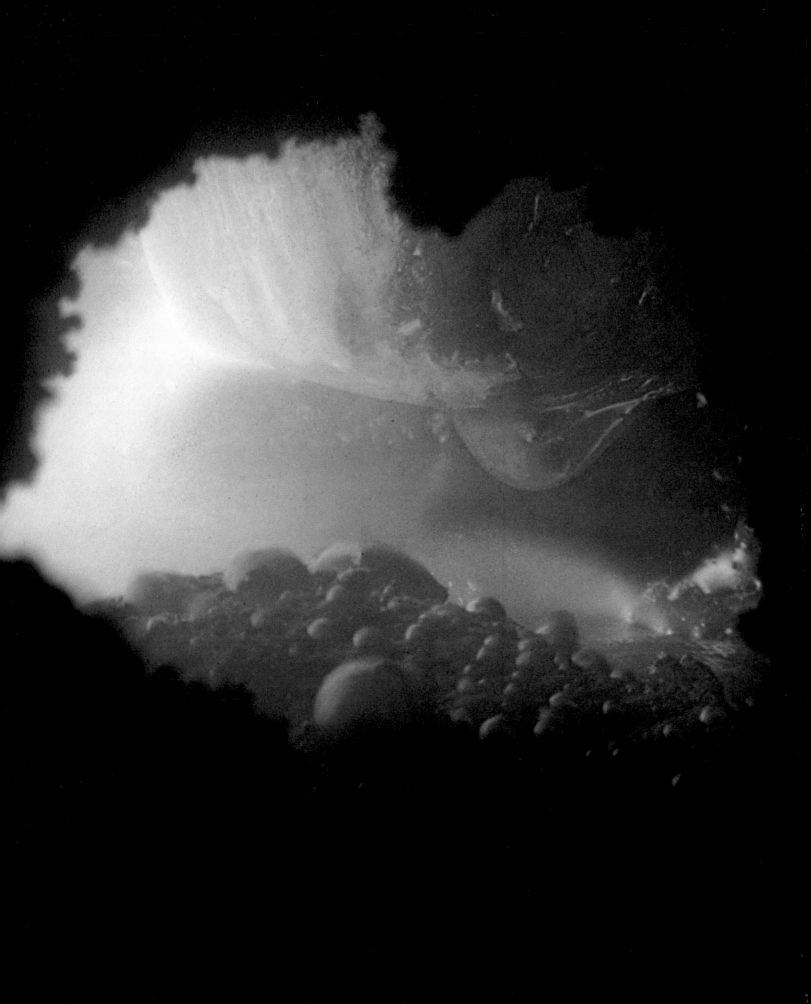

The expansion of the Norwegian aluminium processing industry continues at a high rate. Most of the Norwegian-produced unwrought aluminium will still be exported, but new Norwegian semis and finished products are gradually entering the market.

Nordisk Aluminiumindustri in Holmestrand, for example, has started construction on a fully-automated rolling mill which will have an annual capacity of 45,000 tons. It will produce aluminium strips in a width of 1.5 metres at a speed of 60 kilometres (42 miles) an hour.

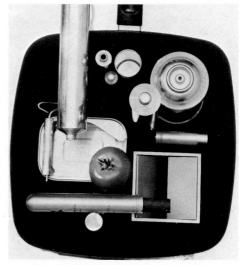

On these pages you will see some of the aluminium products sold by Norway on the world market: semi-finished products from Norsk Hydro, packaging material from Nordisk Aluminiumindustri, pleasure craft from Fjellstrand Aluminium Yachts, and a greenhouse from Raufoss Ammunisjonsfabrikker.

Opposite page. Top left: The newly developed bumper system from A/S Raufoss Ammunisjonsfabrikker has attracted considerable attention from the car industry. By using the Raufoss bumper, car manufacturers are able to meet the new American safety standards.

The ferro-alloy industry represents an important sector of the Norwegian economy. Production capacity has increased considerably and the value of production amounts to about $100 million annually at the present time. More than 90 per cent of ferro-alloy production is exported. Main products are ferro-silicon, ferro-manganese, silico-manganese and ferro-chrome. There are about 4,500 people employed in the country's 13 ferro-alloy plants. Most of the plants are located in less-industrialized areas and some in areas where the local community is entirely dependent on the company.

Meråker is such a community. Meraker Smelteverk *(below)* is not among the largest producers in Norway, but production includes silicon metal, magnesium ferro-silicon, ferro-silicon, low carbon ferro-chrome and calcium carbide. The raw materials limestone and quartz are obtained from the company's own mines.

Photos. Right: The raw material stocks and low carbon ferro-chrome production at Meraker Smelteverk.

From Fiskaa Verk, Elkem-Spigerverket's oldest ferro-alloy plant. The concern's large research station is located here. Fiskaa has four Elkem-Spigerverket smelting furnaces equipped with Søderberg electrodes.

Most of the raw materials for ferro-silicon production are Norwegian, except for the coke. On the other hand, most of the metal produced is exported.

Left: Deformed reinforcing bars are produced in Norway by both Elkem-Spigerverket and Norsk Jernverk.

The re-establishment of an iron and steel industry in Norway was a strong national desire ever since the country gained its independence in 1905. It was not until after the Second World War, however, in 1946, that the time was ripe for the creation of A/S Norsk Jernverk. The construction of the steel works was considered a national task and the company is one of the few state-owned industries in Norway. The decision to build the steel works at Mo i Rana, close to the Arctic Circle, was seen as a measure to strengthen the industrial base of North Norway. In addition, the area possessed sizable iron ore deposits and water power resources.

Norsk Jernverk employs 4,000 people and in 1972 produced 577,000 tons of pig iron, 704,000 tons of steel ingots, and 94,000 tons of tinplates. Total sales amounted to close to $100 million, with exports accounting for 71 per cent. Close to half of the entire output is sold to EEC countries.

Photos: Reinforcing steel and steel for the shipbuilding industry are Norsk Jernverk's most important products.

Production at Norsk Jernverk started in 1955. Further expansions have taken place in stages. In 1965 the company started mining operations covering 80 per cent of the concentrates used by the steel works. The crude ore is extracted on the basis of open-cast mines which contains 33 per cent iron.

FROM TREES TO NEWS

Ever since man first settled on the northernmost edge of Europe, the forests have furnished the material for fuel, for shelter, for boats, thus ensuring the basic means of livelihood. Forestry products are a traditional Norwegian export based on one of Norway's principal natural resources. Lumber exports were one of Norway's main export trades from the 16th century to the beginning of the 20th century, but now the timber goes mostly to Norway's own wood-processing industry. The pulp and paper industry has enhanced the value of the timber, and the manufacture of rayon and other forms of processed wood have also helped to boost the value of every tree felled.
Almost 100 years have passed since Norway first started to export pulp and paper on a regular basis. For many years paper ranked first among the Norwegian export commodities, ahead of fish, metals and other products.
In terms of total world production Norway's output is quite small. According to the latest FAO statistics Norway's exports of pulp and paper represent less than 6 and 5 per cent respectively of world trade in these commodities.
Paper and board represent the major products from Norway's wood-processing industry today. Although the forests cover a quarter of the surface of Norway, topographical and climatic conditions are not propitious for a high timber yield. The rate of growth is relatively slow and considerable tracts of forest are not easily accessible. This is the background for a natural desire to increase the degree of processing in the Norwegian forest industry.
Norwegian paper is exported to more than 100 countries. By 1972 Norway had 39 paper mills with an average production of about 35,000 tons. While these mills are still small compared to the giant North American plants, they are in general considerably bigger than the mills on the Continent.
In the last 20 years the paper and board production has trebled, to about 1.4 million tons a year. The introduction of larger machines and increased specialization have made it possible to raise production with no proportional increase in manpower.
The forests are also an essential source of income for a great many farmers in Norway who combine farming with forestry. In addition, the pulp and paper industry provides employment for thousands of men in districts with few other means of livelihood.

Left: A selection of newspapers and magazines printed on paper from Norway.

Below: The pulpwood stocks at Sarpsborg are used by the Borregaard mill which consumes about 800,000 cubic metres a year. Borregaard is one of the largest industrial groups in Norway. Pulp and paper account for 40 per cent of the company's annual turnover.

Right: In 1971 Borregaard started producing pulp based on eucalyptus trees in Rio Grande Do Sul in Brazil. The pulp is shipped to the company's plant in Norway for further processing. The new plantations in Brazil cover an area of close to 75,000 acres. As the eucalyptus trees are ready for felling after 7 years (compared to 70-130 years in Norwegian forests).

Two major Norwegian paper producers, A/S Union and A/S Follum Fabrikker, celebrated their 100th anniversary in 1973. Not very long ago Follum (below) was a medium-sized wood-processing firm. Today, the company has 1,200 employees and a production of 150,000 tons of newsprint and 42,000 tons of magazine paper annually. Follum's newest paper machine produces 750 metres of newsprint a minute or 45 kilometres (28 miles) an hour.

A/S Union has seven mills employing altogether some 1,600 persons. In addition to the production of special papers and greaseproof, 160,000 tons of newsprint are produced annually.

Opposite: A/S Vittingfoss, one of Norway's 39 paper mills.

This page: Nordenfjeldske Treforedling, a division of Norske Skogindustrier A/S. The company is owned by Norwegian forest owners. At the Nordenfjeldske Treforedling mill in Skogn, which is the largest unit in the Norwegian pulp and paper industry, 220,000 tons of newsprint are produced annually.

Right: The development of efficient and reliable forestry equipment has been particularly important in Norway where forestry plays such a key role. For 25 years, JOBU, a division of the Elkem-Spigerverket Group, has been manufacturing power saws for forestry use in Norway and other countries.

Below: Increased mechanization and new methods of transport have radically altered forestry operations. The horse and sleigh have been replaced by modern machines and equipment.

Next page: Although one quarter of the surface of Norway is covered by forests, Norway generally imports about 40 per cent of its annual pulpwood requirement. Norway is the world's biggest pulpwood importer after Japan.

Improved cultivation methods are being adopted to ensure and increase the future supply of timber. It is estimated that the yield from Norwegian forests can be doubled in 25 to 30 years.

The growth of timber can be increased considerably by using chemical fertilizers and in this field Norwegian forest owners have played a pioneering role. The fertilizers, produced by A/S Norsk Hydro, are spread from airplanes or from equipment on the ground.

Opposite page. Below. Left: The airplanes often use widened forest roads as landing fields.

86

Right: Originally, the rivers represented the natural way of transporting timber from the forest to the mills. Today, however, more and more of the timber is being hauled by truck. Timber floating will soon be a thing of the past.

Below right: Coffee break for the loggers.

FISHING ON THE DOORSTEP

The Norwegian cuisine has its specialities, some of them unique. Particularly when it comes to fish and fish products, the Norwegian cuisine is at its best. It is only natural that food from an unpolluted ocean or a remote mountain plateau is healthier to consume. Apart from the food products that stem from Norway's special traditions, skills and natural resources, there is a growing food processing industry geared to modern requirements.

Norway ranks fifth among the world's fishing nations, accounting for about five per cent of the total world catch. With a coastline of 1,650 miles (half of which is north of the Arctic Circle), the fishing industry is of major importance with catches up to three million tons in the best years.

An annual catch of about 700 kilos per capita entails that Norway is entirely dependent on exporting its fish products. Frozen fish represents the most expanding sector within the fish processing industry with more than a hundred freezing plants placed strategically along the coast, close to the major fishing grounds.

Photos: Left: Skarsvåg on the island of Magerøy, the northernmost community in Norway. This village is located further north than Point Barrow in Alaska.

89

Since ancient times the sea has been a source of livelihood for the coastal population of Norway. There are 70 different fish species found along the Norwegian coast, but only a few are particularly important. The Norwegian fisheries are nevertheless extremely varied.

The Arctic cod has been the basis for the large seasonal cod fisheries. The best known cod fishing takes place in Lofoten during the winter. About 6,000 fishermen and 2,000 boats participate in the Lofoten fisheries from which these photos are taken.

Pages 92–93: Svolvær – the centre of the Lofoten fisheries.

Deep freezing of food has long traditions in Norway and Norwegians have played a central role in developing modern freezing methods.

Norway's geography is the principal factor in determining the exceptional quality of Norway's fish. The rich Arctic fishing grounds lie only a few miles from the freezing plants located along the coastline of North Norway.

The photos on these pages show a few of the more than 150 freezing plants in Norway. More than half of them are located in North Norway.

One of the world's largest fish marketing organisations, Frionor Norsk Frossenfisk A/L, Oslo, is exporting frozen seafood to two dozen countries throughout the world. The Frionor chain of freezing plants has developed from 45 to 122, and annual output has increased to about 70,000 tons. Frionor can boast a remarkable range of 400 varieties of seafood – from tunny and whale meat to prawns and cod roe – and in terms of variety as well as volume Frionor is one of the world's seafood leaders.

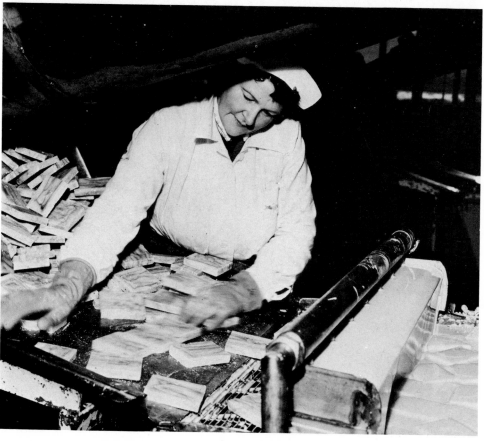

The Norwegian coast is a strip of land both challenging and rich in contrasts. It can be idyllic and charming during sunny summer days when day and night blend into one, but it can also be stormy, bleak and dark during the long winter nights. Work at sea is always demanding in the far north. The weather is never safe for those who harvest the riches of the sea, and as long as Norwegians have lived they have learned the truth of the old saying: The sea gives and the sea takes. Photos can illustrate far better than words the unusual climatic characteristics of life along the coast in the north.

Dried fish (stockfish) is an ancient Norwegian export commodity. After the fish is gutted and cleaned, it is hung up for drying *(top)* until the fish is almost bone-dry. Climatic conditions in North Norway are ideal for the production of stockfish because of the crisp cold air.

Stockfish contains about 80 per cent protein, entailing that one kilo of stockfish has the same nutritional value as five kilos of fresh fish.

Nigeria has always been an important market for Norwegian stockfish. At the market in Lagos *(below)* stockfish is a very popular item.

Fish farming belongs to the future. Previous generations of fishermen have drawn their catches from the sea, while future generations will breed fish in controlled environments. Salmon breeding on a large scale is still a new industry, but the idea of using the Norwegian fjords for the mass production of salmon is no longer distant fantasy from a science fiction novel.

Below: One of the two salmon hatcheries operated by A/S Mowi near Bergen. The water in the hatchery can be heated to hasten the growth process. Fresh water and sea water are pumped into the tanks and in this way the fish can gradually be prepared for transfer to salt water. Later, the spawn are transferred to sea-water installations where, after two years, the salmon reaches a marketable size of about 3 kilos *(above)*.

Norway's canning industry has a production of about 50,000 tons of canned fish a year, of which about half is brisling and sild sardines. The other half consists of a great variety of products. Exports are widely distributed.

On the production side, Norwegian canners are co-operating in building and operating vessels that can be deployed in various waters, catching, freezing and transporting the enormous quantities of sardines required by the industry.

Previously, the canneries were only in operation on a seasonal basis, but large deep-freeze storage facilities for raw materials now make it possible to operate all through the year.

Chr. Bjelland & Co. A/S, Stavanger, is Norway's biggest fish canning concern with 12 factories employing some 1,200 persons.

Norway's fish canning industry has stimulated the development of new designs in canning machinery. Trio Maskinindustri secured important orders from the USSR for several complete production lines.

Photos: Norwegian delicacies on the world market.
Below: Norway's canning industry co-operates in research and quality control and runs its own canning school in Stavanger.

A large part of the Norwegian fish catch is reduced to meal. As a fish meal producer Norway ranks second in the world, surpassed only by Peru.

A fleet consisting of some 600 purse seiners is engaged in the catch equipped with the most modern detection devices, echo sounders and asdics, along with modern ring nets and power blocks.

The utilization of herring as an industrial raw material started in Norway as early as 800 A.D. A very primitive process of pressing the oil out of putrefying herring by means of wooden boards and stones was employed. The residue was occasionally used as fertilizer.

Norway has today about 75 fish meal factories. All along the Norwegian coast factories are ready to convert the catch into oil and meal. The meal is essentially a protein concentrate, since protein accounts for practically ¾ of its total weight.

Opposite page bottom and this page top: The net winches from Aukra Bruk A.S. do the work of many men. The use of power blocks has made it possible to increase the efficiency of fishing operations. The purse seines employed today are large enough to encircle the Oslo City Hall in one throw.

Bottom: One of the 75 fish meal factories along the Norwegian coast.

The Norwegian mountains represent more than a national treasure. Their glaciers and water, waterfalls and rivers have also made them a source of energy in the Norwegian economy. Water power converted to electricity was a prerequisite for many important Norwegian export industries.

The supply of fresh water represents one of the greatest problems of this century. In a recent report dealing with the fresh water supply in West Germany, it is stated that all available ground water resources in the country will be exhausted by the year 2000. 98 per cent of the world's water resources is unsuitable as drinking water. Increasing water pollution, rising water consumption in manufacturing and the population growth make the water supply problems an international issue.

Pure drinking water is thus not to be taken for granted today. Everywhere, pollution is creating difficulties in safeguarding the supply of drinking water. Several Norwegian companies have in recent years started to market Nowegian drinking water and some of them have already found export markets for this product.

The mountains, steep hillsides, the long hard winter and the fact that one fourth of the country lies beyond the Arctic Circle do not exactly offer the most ideal conditions for farming in Norway. The most important agricultural areas are located in the lowlands, but mountain farms at altitudes up to 3,000 feet above sea level can also be found.

The typical Norwegian farmer is a smallholder, but there are also a number of larger farms using the most modern and advanced machinery and equipment.

200 Norwegian dairies produce 50 different varieties of cheese. Norwegian cheese is exported to more than 20 countries, with Japan as the largest customer. Norwegian blue cheese *(left)* is primarily produced in the Trøndelag district. Jarlsberg cheese *(right)* is based on an ancient recipe from the Jarlsberg estate on the western shore of the Oslo fjord.

Below: Livestock provides 75 per cent of the income in Norwegian agriculture. In addition to 420,000 cows, Norway has more sheep than the four other Nordic countries combined.

HOMES FOR GRACIOUS LIVING

A dwelling reflects a way of life, personality and living conditions. Because Norwegians are compelled to spend a great deal of time inndoors, they place special emphasis on houses and cottages which are both attractive and functional. Naturally, a large share of the population is concentrated in blocks of flats in the larger towns, but most Norwegians still seem to prefer owning a small house of their own. Most houses are made of wood, but the use of wooden materials is combined with modern insulation, double glazing, efficient heating and comfort. The houses are equipped for all the seasons of the year and the houses built in Norway must therefore be more sturdy than those in warmer climates. Norwegians often claim, in fact, that they are never so cold as when they experience winter outside their own country. Norway's natural surroundings providing almost unlimited possibilities for relaxation and outdoor living place the country in a privileged position in a heavily populated Europe. The Norwegians' craving of the sun and enthusiasm for outdoor life explain why 40 per cent of all Norwegians have a second home which they own or share with their family. Some families even have two second homes, one for the summer and one for the winter. Most of the holiday homes, whether located in the mountains or by the sea, are simple and inexpensive without any luxuries. They vary in size and design, from small huts for hunters and fishermen to large country estates. In recent years the authorities have adopted laws prohibiting the development of holiday areas within a 300 yard strip along the coast in order to preserve access to the seashore for all tourists and boatowners.
Still, there is sufficient room for additional thousands of holiday houses. More and more of the Norwegian houses are prefabricated.
There exist about 230 companies in Norway in this field today. Most of them are small, but some important prefabricated housing manufacturers have also managed to develop considerable exports.

Left: Housing area built from prefabricated elements. Erected by Ringsakerhus, member of the Moelven Group.

A/S Moelven Brug was established in 1899. During the last twenty years the company has undergone many changes and a rapid growth, and is today the parent company of the Moelven Group with a product line ranging from modular houses, mobile house units, and building panels to trailers and cranes. Total sales of the Group amount to about $33 million.

During the last decade heavy emphasis has been placed on research and development in the building industry. The process has led to an extensive interest in prefabricated houses and the company has developed considerable know-how and skill within the field of industrialized housing. Moelven offers a total of 250 types of prefabricated houses.

Photos: Parts of the interior of the Moelven modular housing plant at Moelv. In the foreground we see the erection station for the modules. The floor, walls and roof panels are transported from their stacking conveyors. The floor panel is positioned at the erection station by pneumatic stearing gears. Two end-wall panels are then automatically placed on the floor.

The sections are transported from the factory to the building site. It only takes a short time to assemble the sections and then the house is ready for occupancy.

Half of the 15,000 one-family houses which are built annually in Norway are prefabricated. One of the largest producers is the Block Watne Group which in 1972 supplied 2,600 houses. In terms of architectural design, quality and production techniques, Block Watne is well prepared for the future.

In addition to its production of houses, the company has recently expanded into the fields of prefabricated day nurseries, homes for the handicapped, homes for the elderly and schools.

Block Watne has also started to export to a number of countries.

Opposite page: Top: During recent years the Block Watne Group has concentrated heavily on research and development in the housing field.

Bottom: The big advantage of prefabricated houses is the short time needed for construction. The house is completed one week after the sections are brought to the building site. At Block Watne's new production plant, covering about 215,000 square feet, the floors, walls and roof are joined to form sections before they leave the factory.

This page: There are 43 standard types of Block Watne houses.

For generations the Norwegians have perfected the wood-working arts, and it is said that they are the world's finest timber craftsmen. Trybo homes are designed to withstand the extremes of the Norwegian climate and many houses in Norway built from identical types of timber are over 800 years old.

The Trybo holiday homes are manufactured by A/S Trybo, a company owned by the forest municipality of Trysil. The company engaged leading architects to design both the cabins and the interiors. Trybo has won notable awards abroad as well as in Norway.

Based on a 39 inch module, the Trybo homes are produced in three widths, 13, 16 and 19 feet, and the system is flexible to allow for a great variety of shapes and sizes.

The homes are fully insulated for Norwegian high-mountain conditions and the windows are double glazed. Norwegian pine and spruce have been used as construction materials so that these holiday homes harmonize well with their natural surroundings.

These pages show some of the holiday homes produced by Trybo. The Swedish magazine 'Femina' characterized Trybo as 'the house you fall in love with' and the Danish magazine 'Bo Bedre' awarded the house a gold medal as the year's best holiday home.

In a country with a varied landscape and climate there will always be a need for a number of different types of cottages and second homes. Naturally, the construction and design of a cottage in the mountains must be different from a summer house by the sea. It is often quite difficult to combine these requirements, but among the many holiday homes to be found on the market today, there is a second home for every need and preference.

Block Watne has developed the element cottage 'Troll' shown on this page. None of the elements weighs more than 50 kilos and it is so simple to assemble that even the owner can do it himself.

116

Page 117: Norwegian furniture has become an important export article during the last decade. Chairs from Westnofa Ltd., Sunnmøre.

Working in wood is a native skill that has been handed down for generations in Norway and the quality of Norwegian furniture workmanship is recognized internationally. This is also reflected in successful world-wide sales.

Norway's furniture industry consists of many small units, ensuring that traditional craft standards are maintained. According to a 1969 survey there were 574 furniture-makers in Norway. Only 35 of them had more than 50 workers.

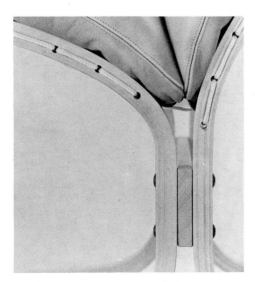

As a small country, with so many small manufacturing units, Norway seeks to compete by virtue of design and workmanship rather than by trying to sell large quantities of cheap, mass-produced furniture.

Norway's furniture industry offers many styles, from traditional and rustic to modern and sophisticated. The most popular models come under the category of internationally acclaimed Scandinavian design. There is also a new generation of rustic furniture, built in native pine, shaped simply and functionally for modern living. Popular for country cottages, it also fits easily into modern town flats and houses.

It is often said that one good way of becoming acquainted with the distinctive flavour of any particular country is to study its arts, its crafts and its industrial design. And there is a good deal in this notion; the things people use in their daily lives often give an excellent indication of the way they live and think.

Photos: Top right: The traditional craftsman's ideals have been especially apparent in the production which modern Norwegian industry offers for the home. When the long winter evenings come, the Norwegians retreat indoors. Consequently, they fill their homes with lovely things as shown here; teapot from Figgjo Fajanse-Stavangerflint A/S, satin steel Maya cutlery from Norsk Stålpress A/S and goblets from Hadelands Glassverk.

Below: The production of beautiful articles in gold, silver and pewter is an old-established Norwegian craft.

Next page: Outstanding design is characteristic of the handcrafted PLUS products, which must be approved by a jury before being released on the market.

LEISURE AND PLEASURE

The very marked seasonal variations in the climate have, of course, exercised a major influence on the whole pattern and rhythm of life in Norway. Throughout the winter large parts of the country are covered with snow, and the hours of daylight are limited. Even in the extreme south there are only some six hours of daylight at mid-winter and the north lies in total darkness. But Norway is a country of sharp contrasts. To make up for the harsh winter, the summer months provide long hours of daylight. In the north the dazzling beauty of the Midnight Sun compensates for the winter murk.

The Norwegian summer can be warm and pleasant, but sun and warmth cannot be taken for granted in a country so far north, where some of the inhabitants live closer to the North Pole than anywhere else on earth. As a result, the approach of spring and summer is perhaps welcomed more enthusiastically by the Norwegians than by many people living further south where sunshine may be more of an everyday occurrence.

Because the country has no large cities, the four million inhabitants enjoy an easier access to nature than most people living elsewhere in Europe. This influences leisure time activities and Norwegians of all ages try to take advantage of the available opportunities for outdoor recreation as often as they can.

The long coastline made Norway a seafaring nation. The sea was the natural means of communication and boating was a necessary element of everyday life for many. Today the pleasure boat fervor has spread and the coast draws flocks of boatowners each summer. There are more than 200,000 pleasure boats in the country and soon every fifth Norwegian family will have a boat.

Photo: Not everyone migrates to the coast during the summer. Popular pastimes include hikes through forests and fields where there is still enough room for everyone to find his own path and experience the peace and tranquillity of nature. The photo shows Liggeren in Nordmarka outside Oslo.

123

Norway's rivers are a paradise for salmon anglers and each year enthusiastic sports fishermen from all over the world pay enormous sums for the right to fish salmon. While salmon fishing may be a sport only a few can afford, Norway's close to 300,000 good fishing lakes and a network of rivers and streams ensure that fishing is a sport which can be enjoyed by everyone. A fishing licence is required and in 1972 300,000 Norwegians and foreigners paid for such permits.

Top left: Mustad is a name known to anglers all over the world. The production line includes some 60,000 different hooks,

from tiny hooks of some millimetres to big ones measuring more than a foot.

Opposite page. Top right: A proud young fisherman.

Bottom: A pleasant combination of fishing and relaxation.

In view of the increasing number of pleasure boats, stricter safety regulations are required. The Norwegian classification society Det norske Veritas has its own department for supervising the building and moulding of reinforced plastic boats. This supervision aims at greater safety at sea for small pleasure craft. The society has formulated special rules for the construction. Boats certified by Det norske Veritas have been tested and approved to meet a large number of safety regulations.

Below: Pleasure craft being tested at Det norske Veritas' headquarters in Oslo.

Opposite page: 'Yngling', 'firling', 'soling', 'gambling', 'mekling', 'fjordling', 'willing', 'smiling', 'brisling', 'tromling' – all boats ending with 'ling'. Ling stands for Norway's foremost pleasure boat designer Jan H. Linge and is his trademark for the various types of boats he creates. Linge is world renowned for his pleasure boats. The Soling Class is today international and is raced in the Olympics. So far 2,000 Soling boats have been licence-produced in 15 countries. Jan Linge has designed a number of other sailboats as well, from the smallest types to the 34 ft. ocean-going 'Gambling'. In addition, he has created several very popular motorboats sold on the international markets.

«Mekling» *(opposite page)* is one of Jan Linge's new designs, a boat which may establish a new trend as several of Linge's previous designs have done in the past. «Mekling» is manufactured by Kristiansand Mek. Verksted A/S.

Top left: «Robust» 21 ft. motorboat produced by Fjordplast, Norway's largest manufacturer of pleasure boats. The company also offers ocean-going sailboats, luxury cruisers and speedboats.

Bottom left: A late summer evening on the southern coast of Norway with a «Draco» boat from Kåre Drangsholt, Flekkefjord.

Above: With Max Trimaran on a crab hunt.

Below: Sun and summer in the southern part of Norway, the Norwegians' favourite spot for summer holidays.

Right: It's not strange that a pleasure boat ranks so high on the list of preferences in a country where most people live close to the sea and feel an intimate attachment to it.

This is the Norwegian dream: a summer evening with friends and family, a bonfire and picnic basket on the beach, with a boat anchored nearby. The boat is a «Saga 27» built by Selje Bruk A/S. Such a vessel is more than a means of transportation. It is ideal for summer cruises among islands and reefs – the perfect way of spending a holiday according to many.

Opposite page: Heading for a summer adventure.

Left: From the European championship regatta in the Soling class, Hankø, 1970.

Below: Summer at Svenner Lighthouse.

The mountains are an attraction, in summer as well as winter. They are popular for hunting in the autumn, fishing during summer nights or simply for hiking to enjoy nature and relax in the pure mountain air.

Norwegian industry has developed equipment for hunting, fishing, camping and hiking in response to the needs. Hunting and hiking outfits, boots, sleeping bags, tents and rucksacks are indispensable items on mountain trips.

Norwegian equipment in this field has been selected for use in mountain climbing expeditions to the Himalayas and the Andes and is popular among outdoor people in many countries all over the world.

The photos show hunting outfits from Helly-Hansen A/S and camping equipment from Norrøna Sportsartikler A/S.

Next page: View from the top of Norway. The country's highest mountain, Galdhøpiggen, rises to a little over 8,000 feet.

We are living at a time when people in most industrialized countries understand the importance of exercise and physical fitness. Sedentary office work and hour-long car trips make it essential for the human body to have a daily dose of exercise.

The development has brought the bicycle back to our everyday life, both as a «bodyguard» in the home and as a means of transportation for leisure time activities.

Jonas Øglænd A/S has a dominating position as a bicycle manufacturer in Scandinavia. An entirely new bicycle factory in Sandnes, covering and area of more than 250,000 sq.ft., will enable Øglænd to enter new markets, including the U.S. where the bicycle is really «in». Øglænd's bicycle production has increased rapidly. It took 45 years to manufacture the first million bicycles, but only three years to produce the last.

It is highly important to stimulate and develop a child's creativity and imagination. The designer Svein Mortensen of the design centre PLUS in Fredrikstad has been studying this question. On this page we see the plastic play units he has created for Norsk Teknisk Porselenfabrikk. The units can be bolted together to form exciting tunnels and houses, swings and tables for work or play. The set has been tested successfully in a number of nursery schools and play parks, and is particularly suitable for children playing in groups.

WINTER FOR FUN

There are only just under four million Norwegians, but in the winter sports world they have played a role that is quite outstanding. Skiing particularly is a sport that Norwegians have spread world-wide. Practically all ski disciplines, from spectacular jumping to invigorating cross-country touring, stem from Norway.

In Norway, skiing is certainly a spectator sport, and contests on the local, national, and international level draw large crowds. But it is also a sport that is actively practised by hundreds of thousands of Norwegians, men, women and children, who with small towns and large open spaces enjoy the easiest possible access to mountain slopes and forest trails.

A northern country, a mountain country, a forest country, Norway provides the ideal environment for winter sporting. Even the capital, Oslo, is ringed by hills and woods, snow-covered for months during the long winter, that can be reached in under half an hour.

The typical Norwegian form of skiing is cross-country or touring. Norwegians have long regarded cross-country skiing as the best tonic against modern stress, and now abroad, in Central Europe and North America particularly, great numbers of people are also taking up cross-country skiing for the same physio-psychic reasons – to get fit, and stay fit, in body and mind.

Left: Ski vacations in the mountains are part of the Norwegian way of life.

Below: There are indications that skiing dates back 4,000 years in Norway. The Øvrebø Ski, which is 2,500 years old, was found in the southwestern part of Norway in 1929.

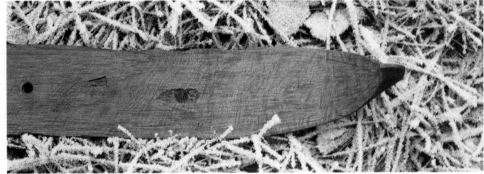

Below: It has been said that the Norwegian is born with a pair of skis on his feet. This is naturally a slight exaggeration, but age doesn't count too much when a child experiences his first ski trip seated in a pulk sledge as his parents pull him along the trails of the forests and mountains.

A little later the child must stand on his own two feet. Only practice makes perfect. It is common to give children skis for Christmas when they are about 3 years old, and it doesn't take too long before the toddlers are skiing along with their parents on hour-long ski trips on winter weekends.

Above: Ski classes are arranged in all parts of the country. Ski instruction is just as much a part of a Norwegian child's education as primary school.

Next page: Winter charm in Oslomarka.

Young enthusiasts – enjoying life.

Each country has its specialities. Norway has skiing. There are about 1,400 ski clubs in the country and on a Monday morning during the winter the sports pages of Oslo's newspapers are filled with the results of the weekend's numerous ski meets, often numbering 50 with about 4–5,000 participants!

Even though there are thousands of Norwegians actively participating in cross-country races, slalom competitions and jumping events, the hundreds of thousands enjoying a leisurely ski tour through the forests and mountains are more representative of Norway as a skiing nation.

Skiing has been practiced in Norway for several thousand years. Modern skiing, however, only dates back to the middle of the last century when some ingenious skiers from Telemark developed new and revolutionary ski bindings. For some time Norway seemed to have a monopoly of skiing and the word itself was virtually unknown in other countries for a good part of this century. The first reports outside of Norway on the Norwegians' dexterity on skis related to jumping. Foreigners read with amazement about Norwegians who could fly through the air with a pair of «wooden wings» attached to their feet. But sportsmen in other countries learned quickly and today the pupils are often better than their teachers in many fields, even though skiing is still Norway's national sport.

Ski fashions and styles changed through the years. Long, heavy skis were replaced by new lightweight equipment. The simple toe strap made of birch branches was replaced by modern efficient bindings, and heavy fur outfits and clothing which hampered movement were discarded. Today, old and young alike use lightweight clothing for skiing.

The type and design of equipment and clothing made for skiing in Norway today are based on years of practical experience and a large, quality-conscious domestic market. On this basis Norwegian manufacturers of cross-country skis and ski equipment have found new and expanding markets abroad, and have contributed to making skiing a popular pastime all over the world.

Even in the early part of the 20th century skis were both functional and indispensable in many areas of Norway. Skis were used for hunting in the forests and mountains; Doctors could ski for miles to reach their patients and ministers often had to resort to skiing to arrive at the church in time for the sermon. Even members of parliament sometimes needed their skis to reach the parliament building in the capital.

Opposite page: The mountains lie within reach of most Norwegians.

Below: The capital has its own forest eldorado, Nordmarka. On a Sunday during the winter 100,000 Oslo residents use the ski trails which crisscross this 460 sq. mile area. A network of lighted ski trails for evening skiing has also been installed. The photo shows Tryvannsstua, located just half an hour away by car from the centre of Oslo.

The stretch nylon suits for skiers and skaters made by Odlo Fabrikker A/S have had a remarkable international success. These were the first of their kind, and Odlo continues to maintain its leading position. Participants from 23 countries wore Odlo training suits at the 1972 Winter Olympics in Japan.

The photo at top right shows a cross-country skier wearing an extra-light one-piece racing suit, specially treated for minimum air resistance.

There is in fact very little that Norway cannot offer in the winter sportswear field. This is, after all, a field where Norwegian clothing manufacturers possess special knowledge, experience and even flair, making it possible for them to compete successfully on the international markets. The clothing industry has developed winter sportswear as one of its major specialities. The fact that so many Norwegians are active skiers has made ski-wear production a highly competitive business. Thousands of skiers know exactly what kind of clothes are best suited for winter sports. They expect garments that are attractive and stylish, but they also insist that garments must be practical and functional for their purpose

The sportswear manufacturers offer designs in the latest styles, but garments in traditional Norwegian styles and patterns continue to be highly appreciated abroad.

Photo: 100,000 tonner «Ruth», owned by Hagbart Waage, on her way to the Persian Gulf to pick up oil for Europe.

SAILING THE SEVEN SEAS

Income from shipping has played an important role in the development of the Norwegian society. Norwegian shipowners have always been forced to rely on their own personal initiative and energy in competing for cargo on the world markets. No subsidies or special protection from the Norwegian authorities are extended to Norwegian shipping. The merchant fleet operates on all Seven Seas and Norway accounts for 9 per cent of the world's merchant fleet. 90 per cent of all Norwegian ships are engaged in traffic between foreign ports. These ships carry all kinds of cargo: ore from Africa and Australia to Japan, grain from Canada to China, general cargo between Europe and the Far East, copra from Indonesia to the U.S., but above all, oil to cover the growing demand throughout the world.

In order to maintain its competitive position the Norwgian fleet is continuously being modernized. In 1973 more than 50 per cent of the ships in the fleet were sold before they were 5 years old. Larger ships are taking over bulk cargoes such as oil, ore and grain and new specialized vessels are also being introduced. There are carriers for liquefied gas and cars, container ships, roll-on/roll-off ships and, of course, luxury cruise ships, a new expanding field for Norwegian shipowners.

Only Liberia, Japan and Great Britain have larger merchant fleets than Norway. The Norwegian fleet now totals about 22.6 million tons and tankers represent about half of this total. At the beginning of 1973 Norwegian shipowners had placed orders for contracts for 43 new tankers over 200,000 tons. Norway will therefore continue to play an important role in transporting oil to various parts of the world.

The considerable investments involved in the construction of very large crude carriers have necessitated a reduction in the time required for cargo handling. The large tankers load in oil ports located in remote areas far from civilization or ba-

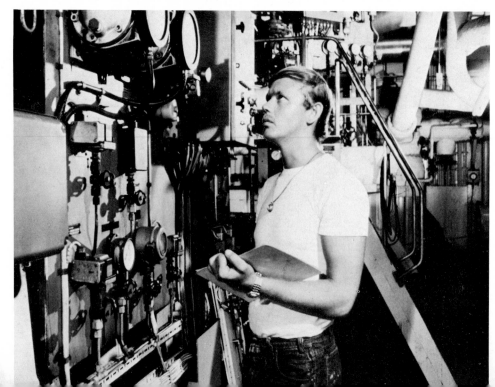

rely within sight of the coast, and they unload in special oil ports located far from the large towns. The entire loading and unloading process takes only a few hours and then the ships head for the open sea again. This doesn't leave the crew much time to go ashore except during their annual home leaves, paid for by the shipping companies.

In order to combat the monotony, a varied programme of activities is provided for the crew and the range of sports activities practiced by the sailors is impressive. World-wide football series are played and sports contests are arranged for everyone. The size of a modern tanker also makes it possible to run a 100-yard dash. A 280,000 ton tanker actually has a length of more than 1,100 feet.

The photos on these two pages give an indication of the everyday life onboard a modern tanker, a life which includes the work involved in operating a ship and relaxation during time off.

Even though cargo liners comprise only a small share of the country's fleet, the liner services occupy a special place in the hearts of most Norwegians. Cargo liners are engaged in scheduled service both to and from Norway and between foreign ports. Liner operations have been particularly adversely affected by flag discrimination and the Norwegian liner companies have encountered many difficulties during recent years. The most well-known Norwegian liner company Wilh. Wilhelmsen operates regular services in many countries. The Wilhelmsen ships, which are shown on these pages, give some impression of the range of world-wide operations of Norwegian liner services.

On this page we see two of the Wilhelmsen Company's cargo liners loading in Malta and Hong Kong. The photos on the opposite page are from Sydney (upper left), Hamburg (far left) and Oslo (bottom). Oslo is not only the capital of Norway, but is also the country's largest town an its political, cultural, commercial and industrial centre On the opposite page (upper right) two Wilhelmsen-ships in Gothenburg. These vessels – one containership and one roll-on/roll-off ship – are among the highly specialized ships in the Norwegian merchant fleet serving the whole world.

During recent years Norway has developed the world's largest fleet of modern cruise ships. Most of these vessels started cruising operations during the last three years, and together they represent an investment of about $300 million. Most of the cruise ships are designed for operations in the Caribbean, but world-wide trips from the Pacific Ocean in the South to the North Cape in the North are also offered.

In 1966 the Norwegian Caribbean Lines started cruise operations from Miami. Today this company has three ships. The company is run by shipowner Lauritz Kloster who started out more than 50 years ago by freighting coal across the North Sea. The Norwegian Caribbean Lines alone transport 100,000 passengers in the course of one year.

Another Miami-based company is Royal Caribbean Cruise Line which has three

sister ships. Royal Viking Line, operating out of San Francisco, also has three ships. The most expensive cruise ship built for Norwegians thus far is the Norwegian America Line's new flagship «Vistafjord», which cost $ 35 million when it was delivered in the summer of 1973. The Norwegian America Line originally had ships engaged in regular transatlantic passenger service, but once the airlines began to take on a greater share of the traffic, the company turned to cruises and cargo traffic.

Top left: A rare rendezvous. Royal Caribbean Cruise Lines' three ships in St. Thomas, West Indies.

Next pages: The average age of the Norwegian cruise ships is 2 years. Here is «Sea Venture», owned by Øivind Lorentzen, Oslo, on her maiden voyage in New York.